A PORTFOLIO OF

KITCHEN IDEAS

HOME HOW-TO INSTITUTE™

CONTENTS

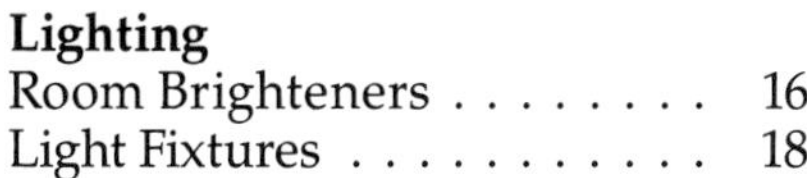

Library of Congress
Cataloging-in-Publication Data

A Portfolio of Kitchen Ideas

p. cm.

ISBN 0-86573-901-3 (softcover)
1. Kitchens — Design and construction
I. Cy DeCosse Incorporated
TX653.P65 1990 90-33946
643'.3 — dc20 CIP

Author: Home How-to Institute™
Creative Director: William B. Jones
Senior Art Director: Brad Springer
Project Manager: Dianne Talmage
Writer: Barb Machowski
Copy Editor: Janice Cauley

Production Director: Jim Bindas
Production Manager: Greg Carlson

Production Art Supervisor: Julie Churchill
Production Staff: Joe Fahey, Kevin D. Frakes, Mark Jacobson, Yelena Konrardy, Linda Schloegel

Color Separations: Colourscans
Printing: Times Offset Pte Ltd, Singapore (0492)

CY DeCOSSE INCORPORATED
Chairman: Cy DeCosse
President: James B. Maus
Executive Vice President: William B. Jones

What makes a great kitchen?

A great kitchen is one that is made just for your family. It is a comfortable, attractive and efficient place in which to work and socialize. Simply put, a great kitchen is a room your family loves.

To help you plan your great kitchen, we have assembled more than 150 color photographs of outstanding kitchen designs and features.

The first section of this book shows how you can customize your kitchen to reflect your family's life-style and tastes. It highlights the elements of a great kitchen: interesting color schemes, unique building materials, creative lighting, space-expanding storage units, and unusual appliances and fixtures.

The second section has more than 50 pages filled with pictures of fantastic kitchens. Included are all the classic styles, ranging from traditional to country to contemporary. We have also added the "inspirational-style" kitchen. This innovative style lets you step beyond the usual boundaries of design and decor to create your own personal look.

Whether you are sprucing up your old kitchen, planning a major overhaul, or designing a completely new kitchen, this book is sure to give you plenty of useful ideas.

Style. *Classic country features such as massive beams and rustic accessories mix well with contemporary tile countertops and flooring. Select a classic kitchen style — country, traditional, contemporary — then give it a personal accent.*

Focal point. *Elegant brass range hood steals the show in this understated contemporary kitchen. Select one stunning feature, material or color, and make it the center of the kitchen plan.*

Color. *Buy a lot of style on a little budget. Accent a neutral scheme with bold, bright accessories, as in this white and red kitchen. A monochromatic color plan is soothing; high-contrast colors are lively and energizing.*

Photo courtesy of KraftMaid Cabinetry, Inc.

Light. *Warm daylight floods the sink area; electric fixture brightens the cooking alcove. Combine natural and electrical lighting in the kitchen plan.*

Photo courtesy of Wood-Mode Cabinetry

Storage. *Pantry has adjustable wire baskets that will accommodate most containers. Swinging panels allow access to back shelves. For efficient storage, use vertical as well as horizontal space.*

Photo courtesy of Kitchens & Baths by Design; David Skomsvold, designer; Ed Cox, Michael Raabe, contractors

Materials. *Rich cabinetry, eye-catching tile and floral wallcovering give this kitchen the feel of spring. The more creative the mix of materials, the more unique the kitchen style.*

Photo courtesy of WILSONART

Detail. *Art Deco kitchen is rich in detail. Curved cabinets and graceful flowers define the period style. Deco colors — peach and green — unify the design.*

PLANNING

Fit your life-style

Kitchen planning starts with a close look at your family. How large is it? Is your family growing? Consider your family's eating and cooking habits. Who eats at home? How often? Does your family eat together? Where?

Think over these questions, too: How much cooking is done each week? Is there more than one cook? Are fresh or prepared foods more important? How often is equipment like a wok, griddle, food processer or pasta maker used? The answers to these questions will help you select appliances and estimate the food and equipment storage space needed.

Include socializing in this life-style inventory. Does your family enjoy entertaining? How often? Where? For how many guests? Is entertaining informal or formal? Do guests help with kitchen duties? A floor plan begins to emerge as you consider how the kitchen relates to the entertaining areas.

Also list special family needs, such as space for a laundry, a sewing and ironing area, a phone center, a hobby counter or seating for children.

Photo courtesy of Armstrong World Industries, Inc.

Plan a home office. *Keep tabs on business from a space-saving kitchen work station. For a unified look, match desk and countertop materials. Here, a computer center in peach and oyster laminate duplicates cabinet and counter materials.*

Photo courtesy of WILSONART

Plan a play area. *Baby is safe in a fenced play yard while Mom or Dad tackles kitchen chores. Plan a carpeted area, located out of the traffic pattern, that is large enough for crawling, toddling and toys.*

Photo courtesy of EXPRESSIONS, A Kitchen & Bath Studio; designed by Lynn Wallace Kelsey

Plan an eat-in kitchen. *Wide granite counter doubles as a table for four, great for meals or snacks. The U-shaped layout simplifies serving and cleanup.*

Photo courtesy of Merillat Industries

Plan for family activities. *Families may cook together, play games or enjoy hobbies in the kitchen. For a successful multipurpose room, plan adequate counter space and efficient storage for non-kitchen items.*

Focus on a great design

Photo courtesy of the National Kitchen & Bath Association

Focus on shape. *Lively angles define this unusual kitchen. The island and light fixture repeat the shape of the triangular room. The practical benefit: space is used efficiently.*

Plan an exciting focal point for your kitchen. Put a ceramic-tile mural in the spotlight, for example, or pine cabinets stenciled with a country motif. Play up an architectural feature in an older home; create interest in a simple contemporary setting by selecting an unusual material for countertops or cabinets.

This bold approach to kitchen design works best if the focal point is planned carefully in terms of scale, shape, color and material. Visualize the kitchen as a complementary setting for the highlighted feature.

Photo courtesy of Armstrong World Industries, Inc.

Focus on a fireplace. *Floor-to-ceiling fireplace is the centerpiece of this contemporary kitchen. Details like a raised hearth, brick firebox, simple mantel and gleaming lamps enhance its appeal.*

Photo courtesy of Wood-Mode Cabinetry

Focus on architecture. *Elegant Palladian window opens up a small kitchen by visually expanding the narrow back wall. The graceful lines of the window echo the rich detailing of the traditional cabinets.*

Photo courtesy of WILSONART

Focus on period style. *Art Deco flowers grow on arched cabinets. The floral design in glass, which is executed in tints popular during the Deco period, defines the color scheme of the kitchen.*

Express your personal style

When you coordinate furnishings, accessories, colors and materials for any room, you express *personal style.* This individual look usually is compatible with a *classic style,* such as stately traditional, lively country, sleek and simple contemporary or "inspirational," an eclectic mix of styles.

Study the elements of classic styles through design books, store displays, design seminars and in consultations with kitchen planners. This step refines planning skills, especially for those who are tackling a kitchen design project for the first time. Then confidently express your personal style.

Contemporary elegance. *Clean lines, neutral or bold colors and simple accents. European-style cabinets characterize the contemporary look. Other popular features include dramatic high-gloss finishes, low-profile appliances and the latest in counter materials.*

Photo courtesy of Dura Supreme

Traditional updated. *Rich wood cabinets are the focus of a traditional kitchen. Look for fine details such as glass doors, pantry storage, decorative molding and high-quality cabinet pulls. Blends well with contemporary colors and materials.*

Photo courtesy of Wood-Mode Cabinetry

Photo courtesy of WILSONART

Inspirational mix. *Country/contemporary. Stark white kitchen is warmed with a wood ceiling, rustic antique dining table and American collectibles.*

Photo courtesy of Armstrong World Industries, Inc.

Country accent. *There's no mistaking this lively style. Rustic cabinets, beamed ceiling and rough-hewn posts echo the interior of a rural cabin. Homespun accessories such as baskets, crocks and willow furniture set the mood. Contemporary-style appliances keep a low profile.*

Photo courtesy of Merillat Industries

COLOR

Pulls a room together

A strong color scheme gives a kitchen character and unifies the design. Consider a monochromatic plan, in which one color, or shades of one color, dominates. Use this color on large areas, such as cabinets, counters or walls.

Set a mood with color. Dark tones bring walls inward, creating intimate space; whites and neutrals open up a room. Warm up a north-facing kitchen with reds, yellows, oranges. Cool a warm-climate kitchen with white, blues, greens.

◀ ***Warm*** *peach walls glow under the recessed lighting. Oak cabinets take on a light wash of color from the warm walls. Soft green, a color complementary to peach, is a subtle accent.*

Photo courtesy of EXPRESSIONS, A Kitchen & Bath Studio; designed by Lynn Wallace Kelsey

Pastels. *Powdery blue-green furnishings set among neutral counters, walls and cabinets create a serene mood. The white ceiling and the wallcovering reflect light, adding a sunny, fresh feel to the room.*

Photo courtesy of Triangle Pacific Corp.

***Cool,** deep blue and dark-finish traditional cabinets set a formal tone. The kitchen is saved from being too dark and sedate by the light-colored flooring and lively geometric wallcovering.*

Photo courtesy of WILSONART

***Brights.** Intense blue packs a lot of color-power in this bold, contemporary kitchen. The blue laminate cabinets are softened with oak trim and light-colored walls and counters. Select dominant colors carefully, since they often will set the tone for adjoining rooms.*

Color

Creates visual impact

Photo courtesy of Armstrong World Industries, Inc.

Bright yellow *laminate counters accent this kitchen and dining area. Black and white in solids and patterns are an effective mix. Yellow dishes set on white tables create a vibrant contrast.*

For visual impact, use bold splashes of accent color. Intense hues, used judiciously, will heighten the contrast in a color scheme.

Lively accent colors prevent neutral color schemes from becoming too subdued. Areas of strong color may also create eye-catching details in a room that lacks architectural interest.

Photo courtesy of KraftMaid Cabinetry, Inc.

Brilliant red *accents are all curves, adding interest to the simple lines of cabinets, counters and wallcovering. Graceful hanging lamp, round vase and framed poster create a focal point at the table.*

Photo courtesy of Interplan Design Corp.; photographed by DOMIN

French blue *knobs, tambour doors, counter edges and molding give a country look to traditional raised-panel cabinets. Patterns make strong accents, too. Note the plaid wallcovering, bordered with blue molding.*

Photo courtesy of the National Kitchen & Bath Association

Skylights/spotlights. *Two generous skylights allow the sun to flood the U-shaped kitchen. Spotlights on a track high in the vault provide general lighting. A second track brightens the cooktop area and turns a dramatic shine on counter and cabinets.*

LIGHTING

Bright looks for cooking and dining

An effective lighting plan combines *general lighting* with *task lighting.* Examples of general lighting include track lights and recessed ceiling fixtures. Working at the sink, cooktop or counter requires task lighting, such as an under-cabinet fixture.

Natural lighting also is an important part of any kitchen plan. Skylights and openings high in the wall, such as clerestory or greenhouse windows, are superior sources of natural light.

Decorative *accent lighting* is taking a more prominent place in kitchen design. A popular choice: lighted glass-front cabinets.

Photo courtesy of WILSONART

Curved greenhouse windows *span the work stations in an efficient galley kitchen. Cans mounted on a track (not visible) provide general lighting.*

Photo courtesy of KitchenAid, Inc.

Clerestory windows *admit volumes of daylight into this cheerful kitchen. Soft yellow walls reflect the natural light. Attractive accent: lighted cabinet shows off floral china.*

Photo courtesy of EXPRESSIONS, A Kitchen & Bath Studio; designed by Lynn Wallace Kelsey

Elegant French doors *topped by an arched window flood this kitchen with natural light. Centrally located fluorescent fixture with diffusing panel provides plenty of general lighting.*

Photo courtesy of Wood-Mode Cabinetry

Recessed lights *illuminate the island and create glimmering reflections in the hanging cookware. Under-cabinet task lights brighten the countertops and showcase a plate collection.*

Photo courtesy of Quaker Maid, div. WCI, Inc.

Hanging lamps, *a decorative alternative to cans or track lights, illuminate the cooktop and chopping board. Above the cabinets, indirect lighting fixtures bounce light from the ceiling onto fresh greenery.*

Photo courtesy of Crystal Cabinet Works, Inc.

Adjustable lamp *can be set at the proper height for those who prefer to be seated as they work. Pull the cord, and the lamp rises for those who like to stand while working.*

Photo courtesy of KitchenAid, Inc.

Trio of lights *turns the sink area into the focal point of this kitchen. Antique leaded glass windows are flanked by lighted glass-front cabinets. A pair of contemporary recessed lights brightens the counter.* ▶

Photo courtesy of EXPRESSIONS, A Kitchen & Bath Studio; designed by Lynn Wallace Kelsey

Eyeball fixtures, *spaced to shine on the sink, cooktop and the walkway to the refrigerator, provide even lighting. Dramatic accent: glass blocks, lighted from inside the counter, shimmer with swirling patterns of icy light.*

Photo courtesy of Wood-Mode Cabinetry

Photo courtesy of Wood-Mode Cabinetry

Custom lighting. *Fluorescent fixture duplicates the shape of the counter, illuminating a corner sink and two food preparation areas. In its base, opaque glass panels diffuse light. Natural oak frame matches the country-style cabinets.*

◀ ***Recessed cans/under-cabinet fixtures.*** *Concealed lighting under wall cabinets brightens every square inch of the counters. Recessed cans highlight the cherry display cabinets and range hood.*

Materials

The building blocks of personal style

Simplify the process of selecting materials for your kitchen by shopping for one or two basics at a time. Tackle counters or cabinets first. Flooring and wallcovering may come next.

Cabinet shopping, for example, boils down to two basic choices: wood or laminate. Survey cabinet styles, then select your material. Next, define the details, such as door style, finish or color, trim and storage components.

Flooring, wallcovering and counters offer a diverse range of choices. Some of the more contemporary materials include glass block, marble, granite or handpainted tile.

Photo courtesy of Lehman & Jones Kitchen Studio; photographed by Mike Krivit

Wood. *The top choice for cabinets. Oak, maple, cherry and pine are favorites. Dark woods have a formal, traditional look. Mix woods, too: dark, rich cherry cabinets are set off by light maple flooring.*

Photo courtesy of Wood-Mode Cabinetry

Light wood. *Light and natural is the contemporary style in cabinets. Oak cabinets in this monochromatic kitchen are treated with a wash of white stain, minimizing the strong grain pattern.*

Photo courtesy of Wood-Mode Cabinetry

◀ ***Wood trim.*** *Enhance fine wood cabinets with wood pulls and counter trim. Match cabinets and trim, like those in the oak kitchen above, or select contrasting stains or woods for a custom look.*

Photo courtesy of Crystal Cabinet Works, Inc.

Laminates. *Flexible laminate sheets bonded to a substrate, usually particle board, make durable counters and cabinets. An array of dazzling colors and patterns is on the market. Above, dramatic high-gloss black laminate is bonded to curved cabinets.*

Vinyl flooring. *Today's sheet vinyls are available in such a huge variety of colors and patterns, they often set the tone for a kitchen's decor. You may want to choose your flooring first, then select complementary counters, cabinets and wallcoverings.* ▶

Photo courtesy of WILSONART

Solid-surface material. *Man-made sheets, up to ¾ inch thick, rival the good looks of granite and marble. Sheets may be cut and shaped like wood. It is an expensive product, but it is durable and resists stains and burns.*

Photo courtesy of Armstrong World Industries, Inc.

Photo courtesy of Armstrong World Industries, Inc.

Glass block, *once a utilitarian material for basement and bathroom windows, now has a place in high-tech interiors. Glass block transmits light, creates stunning visual patterns and is suitable for structural uses such as the counter base shown above.*

Photo courtesy of WILSONART

Ceramic tile *laid in a bold geometric pattern borders an attractive island. Mix tile sizes and colors to create unusual, lively patterns.*

Photo courtesy of WILSONART

Granite-textured laminate *is cut into strips and applied to curved sliding door. Custom cabinets like this add eye-catching detail.*

Photo courtesy of Interplan Design Corp.; photographed by DOMIN

Marble *is a great material for high-profile areas such as this wet bar. It will withstand a lot of wear and tear while maintaining its beauty.*

Photo courtesy of Quaker Maid, div. WCI, Inc.

Ceramic tile. *Customize counters at a moderate cost with patterned tile, tile borders or designs created from tiles of different sizes and colors. Grout colored to match the tile is easier to clean than white grout. Above, earthy tile with floral insets creates a warm kitchen.*

Photo courtesy of Crystal Cabinet Works, Inc.

Marble tile *in high-gloss black with a fine, white grain makes the island the centerpiece of this two-tone kitchen. Marble is a material that complements both traditional and contemporary decors.*

Storage Ideas

Storage systems in wood, metal or plastic are optional accessories in most cabinet lines. Select storage components that fit your budget and cooking style, then follow these storage principles: (1) Store items at the point of use. For example, locate pots and pans in drawers or on heavy-duty pull-out shelves near the cooktop. (2) Fit storage to the items stored, such as divided cutlery trays for silverware. (3) Use every cubic inch of storage space. Don't waste space between shelves. The kitchen on page 24 includes excellent storage ideas, which are illustrated in the photos below.

Pull-out trays *store cleaning supplies, brushes and nonrefrigerated vegetables in sink base.* ***Tilt-down sink panel*** *turns wasted space into a storage area for pads, sponges and other supplies used at the sink.*

Linen trays. *Shallow sliding trays store linens without wrinkling the fabric. Ideal for tablecloths, placemats and cloth napkins.*

Photos pgs. 24 & 25 courtesy of Lehman & Jones Kitchen Studio; photographed by Mike Krivit

Swing-up shelf *is an ideal way to store less frequently used appliances, like this large mixer.*

Spice pantry and drawer. *Island storage puts spices and cooking ingredients within reach of the cooktop. Spice pantry is a fine example of sizing storage to the containers stored. The pull-out drawer allows full use of a deep cabinet.*

Photo courtesy of Wood-Mode Cabinetry

***Roll-out serving cart** glides out from under counter. The three-tier cart is hidden by a false cabinet door when stored. A space-saving accessory for entertaining.*

***Roll-out table** is a big asset for small kitchens. It doubles as a counter or a table for two. Its lower work surface is ideal for pastry preparation. For storage, the hinged false drawer in the counter is lifted and the tabletop slides in; the table legs fit in recesses flanking the base cabinet.*

Photo courtesy of Wood-Mode Cabinetry

***Bread drawer,** a fixture in kitchens in the days before preservatives, is lined with metal and ventilated to keep bread fresh. Pair a bread drawer with a cutting board to create a handy sandwich bar.*

***Corner cabinet trays** rotate, bringing a collection of crockery into view. The wedge-shaped trays fit exactly on the shelves.*

Round cabinet/sliding doors. *Behind tambour-style doors are curved shelves for pots and pans, which are stored directly below the cooktop.*

Photo courtesy of WILSONART

Round cabinet/hinged doors. *Ultracontemporary island features curved laminate doors with European-style concealed hinges.*

Pull-out appliance drawer *frees valuable counter space. Full-extension slides ensure proper support for heavier appliances.*

Photo courtesy of WILSONART

Appliance garage. *Handsome trio of appliance garages with brass tambour doors saves on counter workspace. Two storage nooks hold coffee-making equipment, while a pull-out swivel shelf houses a portable TV.*

Photo courtesy of Wood-Mode Cabinetry

Multilevel storage. *Pantry with adjustable metal storage baskets is a cook's dream. Every can and package is visible. The tall storage racks in the lower section of the pantry rotate so the shelving behind is easily accessible.*

Photo courtesy of WILSONART

Pull-out pantry *fits neatly into a corner, flush with the laminate desk. Plastic-coated metal storage baskets hung on hooks provide flexible storage.*

Photo courtesy of Wood-Mode Cabinetry

***Island pantry** is a wood variation of the multilevel storage system. Two door racks and the rotating racks inside have space-expanding adjustable shelves. A bonus: narrow shelves at the back of the cabinet are adjustable too.*

Photo courtesy of WILSONART

***Pull-out table** topped with a cutting board is part of a complete baking center. In the upper cabinet are baking supplies, utensil racks, and a mixer plugged in and ready to use. Below the table, attractive wood drawers hold bake ware.*

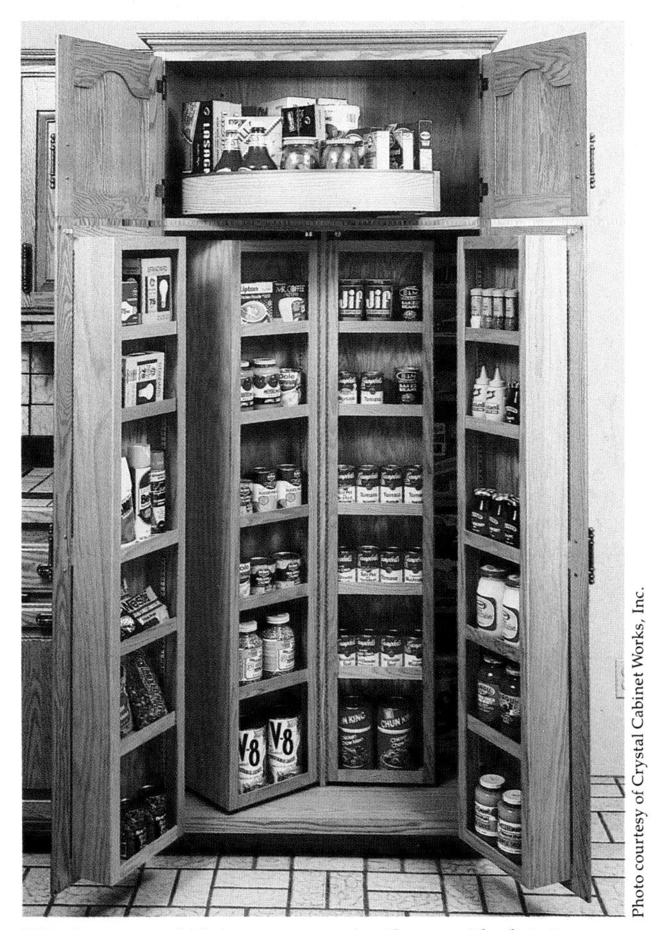

Photo courtesy of Crystal Cabinet Works, Inc.

***Wood pantry,** which is more expensive than most basket storage systems, is a top choice for kitchens with fine wood cabinets. This pantry features a semicircular lazy Susan in the upper cabinet, with adjustable shelves and rotating racks below.*

Photo courtesy of Armstrong World Industries, Inc.

Side-by-side ranges, *shown above, are ideal for large families or for households with more than one cook. Always consider your family's life-style when shopping for appliances and fixtures.*

APPLIANCES & FIXTURES

Today's appliances offer features to fit every life-style. Cooktops with inserts for grills, griddles, deep fryers and rotisseries are available; refrigerator/freezers come in dozens of sizes and configurations; stainless steel and ceramic sinks have one, two or three basins, along with numerous styles of faucets, sprayers and other attachments. Down-sized appliances for small kitchens also are available.

Photo courtesy of WILSONART

Gourmet island. *A budding gourmet can take cooking lessons at this TV/VCR center. With the swiveling TV, the cook can follow recipe directions, in sequence, as he or she moves to work stations around the island. Details: black octagon sink, built-in wine rack, cookbook shelves, multiple storage drawers.* ▶

Photos courtesy of WILSONART

Custom accessories *turn an ordinary kitchen sink into a convenient work center. Cutting board insert, colander and mini drain board are just some of the options available.*

Photo courtesy of WILSONART

Roll-out trash bin *with pop-up lid is concealed within a drawer that matches the cabinets.*

Wine cooler *is a component of a beverage serving center. Other mini-refrigerators are designed for installation in island and base cabinets.* ▶

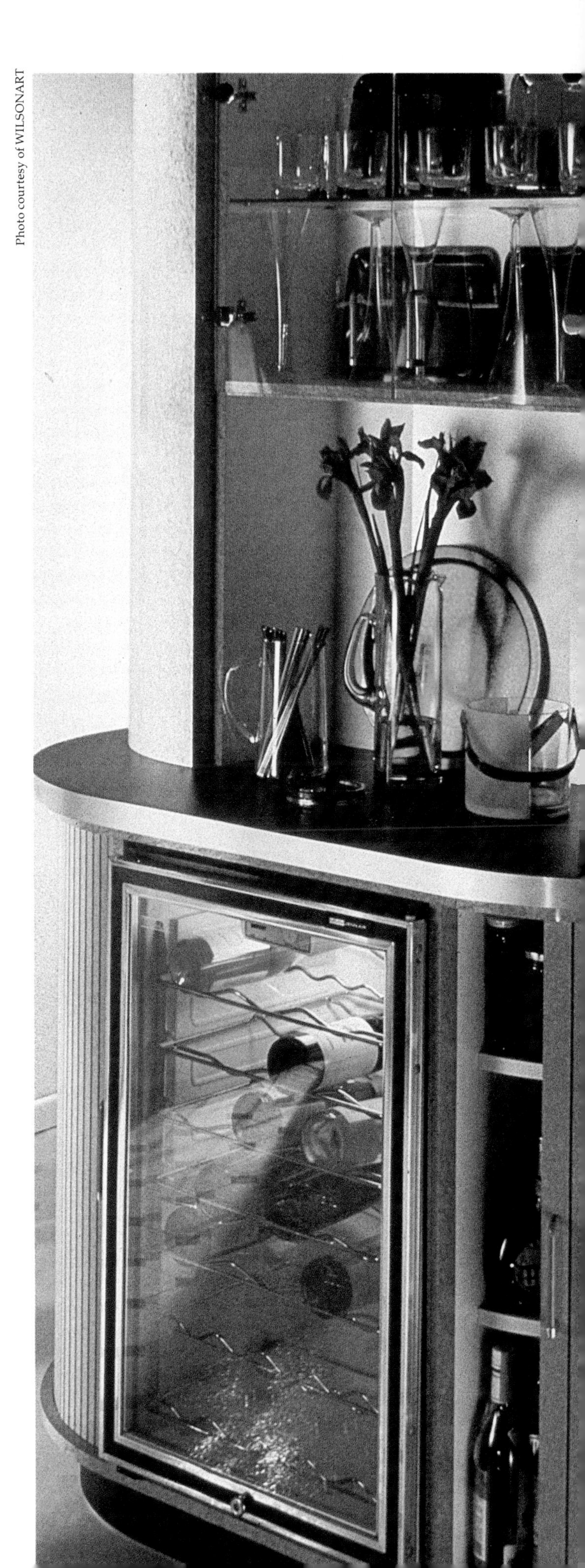

Photo courtesy of WILSONART

Graceful sink *is extra deep for preparing flower arrangements or caring for houseplants. Other uses: beverage service center for a party or a children's water fountain.*

◀ ***Commercial-style range*** *has four high-temperature gas burners, a griddle and a large oven. Textured range hood hides lights and powerful exhaust fans.*

Photo courtesy of Wood-Mode Cabinetry

Photo courtesy of WILSONART

Corner sink *expands design possibilities for the small kitchen. The deep, single-bowl sink is located where it is most useful: between the dishwasher and the food preparation counter. An ideal fixture for a one-cook kitchen.*

Photo courtesy of WILSONART

Microwave/vent hood. *Multipurpose microwave has cooktop task lights and vents in its base. A low-profile vent hood for contemporary kitchens.*

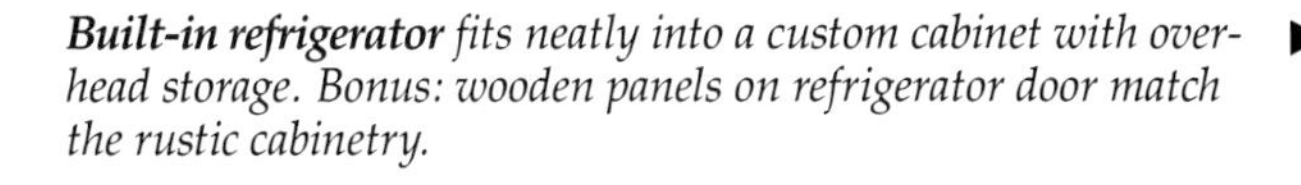

Built-in refrigerator *fits neatly into a custom cabinet with overhead storage. Bonus: wooden panels on refrigerator door match the rustic cabinetry.* ▶

Photo courtesy of Wood-Mode Cabinetry

A Portfolio Of Kitchen Ideas

Elegant TRADITIONAL *Designs*

The traditional kitchen is a showplace for finely crafted wood cabinetry. Oak, walnut and cherry are sought for their distinctive grain. The most popular door styling pairs the cathedral arch wall cabinet with the raised-panel base cabinet. Features like deep crown molding, roomy pantries, open shelving, appliances customized with wood front panels and glass cabinets are hallmarks of traditional styling. Accent with gleaming brass and copper accessories.

Photo courtesy of Merillat Industries

Photo courtesy of Armstrong World Industries, Inc.

***Distinctive double-arch cabinets** dress up this cottage kitchen. Arched ceiling moldings repeat the cabinet pattern. Space-expanding details; salmon and eggshell color scheme, drop-leaf rolling table stored under counter, and floor-to-ceiling cabinets.*

◀ ***Light oak cabinets** blend with the almond laminate counters and ceramic tile floor. Oak is crafted into the counter edge, dishwasher front, appliance garage and distinctive ceiling. Extras like the center island, bar sink, low pastry counter and built-in computer desk reflect this family's life-style.*

Traditional

Details that define the style

▼ ***Two-tier china cabinet*** *is a stunning display case for fine tableware. Curved side panels and inset base reduce its bulk. Traditional accents: leaded glass doors and brass cabinet pulls.*

Photo courtesy of the National Kitchen & Bath Association

Photo courtesy of Wood-Mode Cabinetry

▼ ***Cooktop and grill*** *are set into an opening that resembles a fireplace hearth. Floral ceramic tile unites the island with the cooking area. Pantry is topped with deep molding and dentil.*

Photo courtesy of Crystal Cabinet Works, Inc.

▲ ***Plate rail*** *spans two walls above the oak cabinetry. Along its base are task lights. Brass chandelier with replicas of oil lamps is another traditional touch.*

▼ ***Oversize Palladian window*** *with rich wood trim is the focal point of this U-shaped kitchen. It transforms an ordinary, narrow kitchen into an extraordinary room.*

Photo courtesy of Wood-Mode Cabinetry

Traditional

Photo courtesy of KraftMaid Cabinetry, Inc.

Oak range hood, *which matches the cabinetry in this kitchen, is a handsome way to conceal ventilation fans over the European-style cooktop. Oak spice rack and open shelving have a custom-made appearance.*

Photo courtesy of Quaker Maid, div. WCI, Inc.

Oversize range hood *combines traditional oak with the clean, simple lines of contemporary styling.*

Photo courtesy of Wood-Mode Cabinetry

Crown molding *and a ceiling fan/light fixture add an old-time flavor to this traditional yet very up-to-date kitchen. The roomy kitchen is well suited to the dark cabinets with arched-panel doors and earthy ceramic tile walls and counters.*

***Large island** with durable laminate countertop doubles the amount of space for food preparation. The sink, stove and pantry are within easy reach. Rounded countertop corners and inset double-cabinet base visually reduce its size.*

TRADITIONAL

Islands that fit your life-style

Kitchens of the last century were dominated by a large, central work table. Today, the kitchen island replaces that old-fashioned table. An island expands counter space, increases storage capacity and provides an area for casual dining. Drop in a cooktop with downdraft ventilation, plumb a second sink or wire an electric outlet in the island. For entertaining, invite guests to sit at the island while dinner is prepared.

***Cooktop island** is a snack bar, too. Base cabinets accommodate downdraft ventilation equipment and two storage cabinets. Stools tuck neatly under the almond laminate countertop trimmed with wood. Angled side aids traffic flow around the island.* ▶

Photo opposite page courtesy of Dura Supreme

Photo courtesy of Triangle Pacific Corp.

Brilliant blue laminate *unites the island with the counter behind it. There's plenty of space to set pots, pans and cooking utensils on either side of the island cooktop. Chop ingredients at the butcher block counter, then mix and cook at the island. Stools are out of the way, protected by side panels.*

Photo courtesy of KraftMaid Cabinetry, Inc.

Photo courtesy of Crystal Cabinet Works, Inc.

A contemporary black-and-white color scheme *can work in a traditional kitchen. The trick: use more white than black. Here, handsome black counters and island are balanced with white cabinetry and a sweeping window. Aqua and rattan stools add warm texture and color to the two-tone kitchen.*

TRADITIONAL

Bright looks for elegant designs

Crisp, fresh white gives traditional cabinets a contemporary look. The durable painted surfaces wipe clean easily. A little bit of color goes a long way in an all-white kitchen. Touches like a ceramic tile backsplash, bright cabinet pulls or antique china displayed behind glass doors are strong accents. A must with white cabinetry: white appliances.

Yellow and blue wallcovering *with strong diagonal pattern makes a sunny background for white cabinetry. Deep blue solid-surface countertops blend with the wallcovering. Glass cabinets display a colorful collection of china. White double oven, refrigerator and dishwasher complete the look.* ▶

***Tiny telephone nook** is big on color. Bright aqua cushions accent the black-and-white scheme (see photo, far left). Color details count: notice the cushion piping, striped wallcovering and wall lamp. Overhead cabinets and bench drawers in this charming corner expand storage space.*

Photo courtesy of Crystal Cabinet Works, Inc.

Photo courtesy of KitchenAid, Inc.

Cabinets go light and natural

A new chapter in kitchen design began when traditional cabinets were manufactured with light or natural finishes. Cabinet construction has been updated, too. Many styles are frameless, so doors and drawers fit flush; no cabinet frame is visible. The cabinetry blends beautifully with contemporary patterns and colors in wallcovering, flooring and window treatments.

Photo courtesy of KraftMaid Cabinetry, Inc.

Photo courtesy of Crystal Cabinet Works, Inc.

The most efficient floor plan: *an L-shaped kitchen with island. The refrigerator, sink and cooktop are within easy reach. The solid-surface counters and white ceramic tile island lighten the room. Wood panels camouflage the refrigerator and dishwasher.*

◀ ***Light oak frameless cabinets*** *are pared down to essentials. Gracefully arched window and cooking enclosure complement the straight-line cabinetry. The simple pantry and copper cookware pick up the traditional theme. A space saver: snack bar set below counter height replaces the kitchen table.*

Entertain beautifully *in an elegant kitchen/dining area with matching cabinetry. Oak buffet contains bar sink, glass storage and wine rack for beverage service. Curved kitchen peninsula topped with granite-pattern laminate is convenient for serving and clearing the table. Soft gray wallcovering and flooring unite the area.*

TRADITIONAL

Dressed for entertaining

Photo courtesy of Dura Supreme

Distinctive textures *make this small kitchen a standout. Ceramic tile on walls, counters and floor is mixed with oak cabinets and granite-look laminate table. Traditional details: glass china cabinet, spice boxes and a pantry.* ▶

▼ ***Dress up*** *raised-panel cabinets with molding, flush doors and brass pulls. The rounded edge on laminate counters and above cabinets softens the look. Details like open shelves, a raised serving bar and double ceramic sink with high-rise faucet express personal style.*

Photo courtesy of KraftMaid Cabinetry, Inc.

Photo opposite page courtesy of Kraf:Maid Cabinetry, Inc.

Charming Country Kitchens

Country means comfort, great food, good company. The country kitchen is a relaxed, informal room that combines modern convenience with easygoing charm. Define the style with naturals like pine cabinets, plank flooring, willow baskets and stoneware. Fill your country haven with heirloom quilts and handcarved furnishings or an exuberant display of collectibles. Country mixes well with almost any style, from Victorian to contemporary, so it's easy to modify the look of your home.

__Hefty beams and posts__ set a country mood. Rustic cabinets with wrought-iron hinges conceal the refrigerator and provide storage. An antique woodstove shares kitchen duty with a modern cooktop. Overhead, a lively collection of baskets and cookware.

__Country great room__ spans two stories. The open, airy space easily accommodates a large pine refectory table and comfortable Windsor chairs. A collection of American folk art personalizes the cheerful dining area. ►

Photos pages 50 and 51 courtesy of Armstrong World Industries, Inc.

Updated country kitchen *combines tile counters and rich oak cabinets with massive beams and vintage kitchenalia. Flavor the mix of old and new with whitewashed walls and a cooktop set into a curved alcove.*

Country

Photo courtesy of Dura Supreme

Photo courtesy of Wood-Mode Cabinetry

***Open shelving** extended to the ceiling holds a whimsical mix of kitchen gadgets. Pine cabinets stocked with glassware and serving pieces flank the sink.*

Photo courtesy of Wood-Mode Cabinetry

***Hearty country cooking** requires pots and pans in abundance. A handsome display of gleaming cookware hangs from butcher hooks on a sturdy pot rack above the island. Plate rack shows off Colonial-era pewter dishes.*

Photo courtesy of Wood-Mode Cabinetry

Country

Details define country style. Three ways to get just the right look

◄ ***Use natural materials.*** *Woods like pine, light oak and maple go with the country style. Antique maple butcher block is an all-purpose workspace. Sturdy butcher-block counters are set on primitive cabinets. A wooden paddle fan blends with the pine ceiling.*

Make a color statement. *An eye-catching tile backsplash in warm browns and gray-blue is painted with country designs. Blue molding on the crisp white French-style cabinetry unites the color scheme.* ►

Reproduce a handcrafted design. *Tile patterns resemble stenciling, a decorating technique popular in the 18th and 19th centuries. A stylized vine surrounds the pass-through window. Farm animals decorate the tile walls.* ►

Photos courtesy of Wood-Mode Cabinetry

Photo courtesy of Wood-Mode Cabinetry

Create your own theme

Fresh country. *It's always spring in this pastel-and-white kitchen. Flowers bloom on the contemporary-style wallcovering. A tile border of pale blue garlands accents the counters and walls. High-quality oak cabinets with brass pulls and a pair of rush-seat chairs embellished with flowers set a formal tone.*

◀ ***Barnyard geese*** *wearing floral collars look right at home by the bay window. Large-scale accessories like these life-size animals enhance a theme kitchen.*

Leaded glass cabinets, *brass candlesticks and the sophisticated table setting are worthy of a dining room, yet they fit into this simple, elegant kitchen. Unique range hood unites three design elements: fresh white, blue tile and fine wood.*

Whimsical rabbits, *a traditional symbol of spring, sniff fresh fruit on the counter. A few well-chosen accessories can be as eye-catching as a cluster of small-scale objects.* ▶

All photos pages 56 and 57 courtesy of Kitchens & Baths by Design; David Skomsvold, designer; Ed Cox, Michael Raabe, contractors

ENCYCLOPEDIA

Photo courtesy of Armstrong World Industries, Inc.

Country

Relaxed dining

Why not dine in your country kitchen, close to the aromas of good cooking? Basic ingredients: a generous table and wide, comfortable chairs. Keep the service informal, and add fresh or dried flowers to the table.

Photo courtesy of Wood-Mode Cabinetry

***Garden kitchen** full of windows and plants makes country dining a pleasure. Honey oak table and Windsor chairs match the finely crafted cabinetry. Earthy tile floor warms the neutral color scheme.*

◀ ***Graceful pine table** and cushioned chairs welcome diners to a country gourmet kitchen. The cooking alcove with its striking wood surround holds a double cooktop and side-by-side ovens. A great place to cook a garden harvest feast.*

Touches of blue *and open shelves dominate this understated kitchen. Creamy white cabinets with a low-gloss finish have a subtle shine. Paned glass and scalloped cabinet trim further define the French country look.*

Country

Add a French accent. Mix fresh white, strong blue and gaily colored flowers

Stunning floral mural *grows across the center island. Collector plates repeat the floral theme. White finish on the oak cabinets minimizes the strong grain pattern.* ▶

Photo opposite page courtesy of Crystal Cabinet Works, Inc.

Photo courtesy of Crystal Cabinet Works, Inc.

Fresh-cut wildflowers, *captured in tile, decorate the range hood and wall. Bands of blue enhance the floral pastels. The textured hood surface resembles the white-washed walls found in traditional French country homes.*

Photo courtesy of Wood-Mode Cabinetry

Photo courtesy of Dura Supreme

Country

Classic patterns: plaids and small prints

Victorian influence. *Dark cabinets embellished with dentil molding and lattice cuts are teamed with a handsome parquet floor. Deep-red laminate counters match the striped wallcovering. Classic plaid country curtains dress the tall, narrow windows.*

Photo courtesy of Dura Supreme

Country-modern *kitchen unites contemporary colors and classic cabinetry. Two-color laminate counters and a checkerboard floor dominate the room. Wallcovering and curtain fabric in small-scale patterns coordinate with the colorful accessories.*

Open shelving *stocked with provisions in see-through containers makes a kitchen feel country. Redware and serving dishes are on display in glass cabinets.* ▶

Photo courtesy of Wood-Mode Cabinetry

Photo courtesy of Dura Supreme

Stunning CONTEMPORARY *Designs*

Streamlined describes the clean, crisp contemporary look. The recipe: mix a *minimum* of materials and patterns for *maximum* effect. Sleek European-style cabinets with overlay doors are the top choice for this style. Sophisticated looks combine curving shapes, dramatic color schemes and high-gloss finishes. Color favorites: white and neutrals.

Photo courtesy of Interplan Design Corp.; photographed by DOMIN

***Basic black** polished-granite counters teamed with gray laminate cabinets create a dramatic two-color kitchen. Eye-catching angles: triangular dining counter complements cabinets rising across the wall.*

◀ ***Basic white** laminate cabinets set the stage for bright accessories. Strong black-and-white floorcovering pattern is in scale with the oversize island. Marble-look wallcovering softens a wall of cabinetry.*

CONTEMPORARY

Photo courtesy of Armstrong World Industries, Inc.

Photo courtesy of Crystal Cabinet Works, Inc.

Small kitchen *has handsome tan cabinets that fade into cream walls, visually expanding the room. Streamlined space-savers: appliance garage, built-in refrigerator, and microwave with vent and lights in base.*

Soaring wall *neatly frames the kitchen. Curved counter and simple stools invite guests to perch. An unusual use of pastels in a contemporary kitchen.* ▶

◀ ***Icy glass*** *contrasts with warm peach walls and cabinets in this spacious kitchen/living area. Rounded bilevel counter, chrome stools and cone lights modify the straight-line look.*

Photo courtesy of WILSONART

Photo courtesy of Crystal Cabinet Works, Inc.

Color scheming

Cabinet and counter colors dominate a kitchen, but there are no hard-and-fast rules about *which* color goes *where*. These kitchens demonstrate very different solutions to dual-color design.

Photo courtesy of Wood-Mode Cabinetry

Clean white, warm brown. *White soffits visually extend cabinets to the ceiling. Granite counters provide texture and color. Ultramodern shine: mirrored backsplash, chrome canisters, stainless-steel double sink.*

High-gloss black, soft gray. *Cabinets combine color, shine and curves to create storage as interesting as sculpture. Textured granite counters contrast with the glossy cabinets.* ▶

Photo courtesy of Interplan Design Corp.; photographed by DOMIN

White: pure and simple

White sets the stage. Touches of color, texture and pattern stand out against white cabinets, walls and counters. Complementary elements: white appliances, warm lighting, colorful accents.

Photo courtesy of Merillat Industries

Pure white *shows off the colors of food and flowers. A great kitchen to personalize with accessories in bold colors.*

Focal point. *Gleaming copper and brass hood is the centerpiece of this kitchen, set off by white raised-panel cabinets, white counter and floor. Brass rails and cabinet pulls shine under recessed lights.* ▶

***Subtle textures** of the light gray flooring, counters and wallcovering become important in the minimal kitchen. Another strong element: wide vertical trim that punctuates the wall and base cabinets.* ►

Photo courtesy of KraftMaid Cabinetry, Inc.

***White and gray.** This unusual design pairs white wall cabinets with soft gray base units. Creamy white solid-surface counter unifies the mix. Tableware displayed on open shelves adds subtle color.*

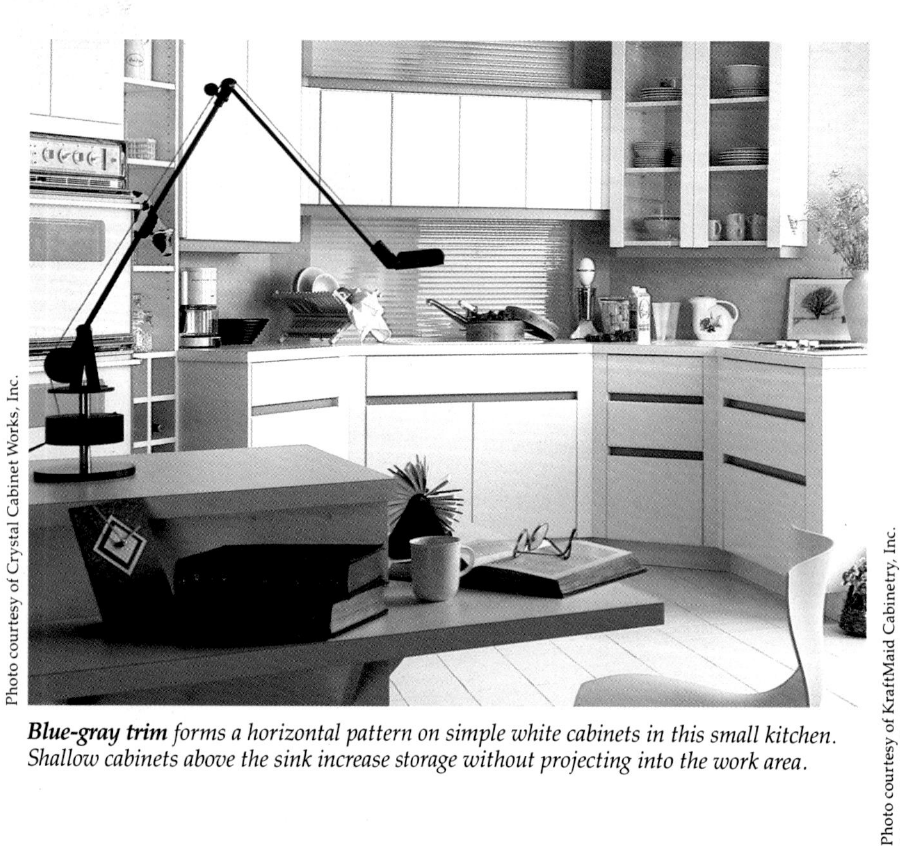

Photo courtesy of Crystal Cabinet Works, Inc.

***Blue-gray trim** forms a horizontal pattern on simple white cabinets in this small kitchen. Shallow cabinets above the sink increase storage without projecting into the work area.*

Photo courtesy of KraftMaid Cabinetry, Inc.

High-style wood

Select wood cabinetry for a warm contemporary look. Sleek European cabinets are available in a variety of hardwoods and stained finishes. Consider other uses of wood: on butcher-block counters, for cabinet trim and pulls, on light fixtures, around windows and doors.

Photo courtesy of Crystal Cabinet Works, Inc.

Combine wood and laminate. *Wood trim on laminate cabinets stands out in this gray and rose kitchen. Matching wood dresses up the appliance garage, bay window frame and lighting fixture over the island.*

Photo courtesy of Wood-Mode Cabinetry

All-wood cabinets. *European cabinets with vertical and horizontal planks are a distinctive alternative to laminate cabinets. Soft-blue tile counter and floral backsplash create the cheerful look of spring.* ▶

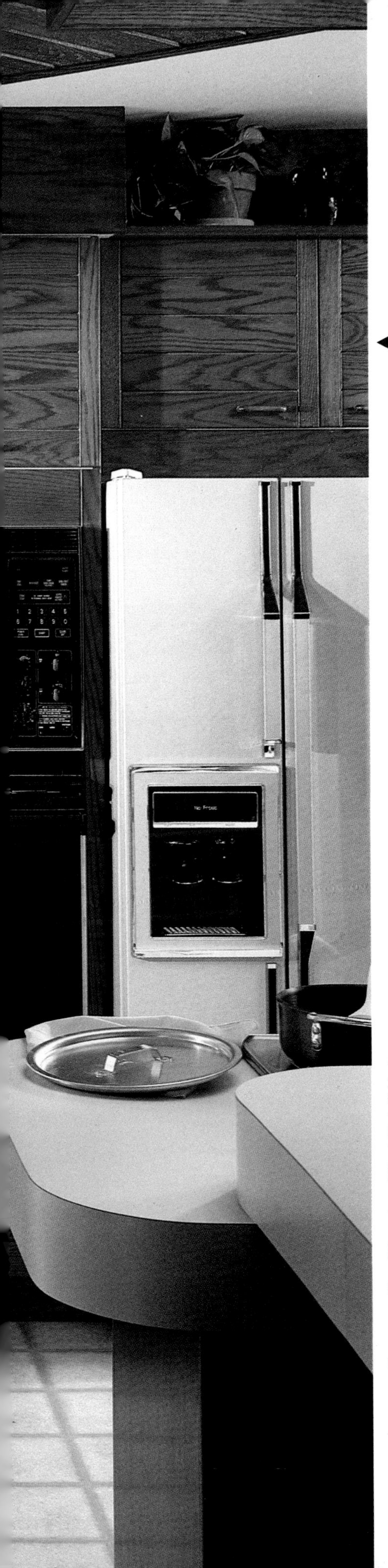

CONTEMPORARY

◀ ***A bold mix*** *of rosewood and laminate creates a light, contemporary cabinet in spite of the dark stain. Rosewood crafted in the window frame, cabinet pulls, corner shelving and plank ceiling unify the design.*

Photos pages 76 and 77 courtesy of Wood-Mode Cabinetry

Contemporary curves *dominate the wood-and-laminate storage wall and multilevel counter. Simple flooring and wallcovering form a neutral background for the high-contrast cabinet materials.*

***Patio door, skylight and window** bathe kitchen in natural light. Supplements to natural lighting: recessed fixtures over island, task lights over sink and cooktop, track lights for general illumination.*

In the right light

CONTEMPORARY

Photo courtesy of Crystal Cabinet Works, Inc.   Photo opposite page courtesy of Quaker Maid, div. WCI, Inc.

Photo courtesy of Armstrong World Industries, Inc.

Balanced light. *Patio door plus window at opposite end of kitchen let the sun in throughout the day. White laminate cabinets and natural light enlarge the small space.*

◀ ***Window wall*** *casts a warm glow over the sink and counters. Flooring and wallcoverings in shades of rust add to the feeling of warmth, which is balanced by light-colored cabinets and counters.*

***Circles and curves** dominate this gray and black kitchen. Multilevel island with vertical laminate is the focal point. Storage wall on the left and cabinetry on right were custom-made for the curved floor plan.*

CONTEMPORARY

Clever curves, smart storage

***Spice racks** recessed into wall below granite-patterned cabinets are close to the mixing area. Detail: sculpted recess in solid-surface panel holds fresh flowers.* ▶

Photos this page courtesy of House Beautiful/WILSONART

Photo courtesy of House Beautiful/ WILSONART

Recessed appliance garages *store coffee-maker, juicer and coffee grinder. Custom-crafted nooks such as these keep counters uncluttered while providing easy access to appliances.*

Sliding door *reveals table linen and silverware storage at the island eating area. Circular cupboard could contain almost any tableware needed for meals.* ▶

Photo courtesy of WILSONART

Photo courtesy of House Beautiful/ WILSONART

Photo courtesy of House Beautiful/ WILSONART

Microwave shelf *provides a space-saving counter for food and dishes. It slides out of the way when not in use.*

◀ ***Lighted glass cabinet*** *houses a collection of delicate sea creatures. Recessed fixtures illuminate the interior shelves. More curves: desk and cabinet side panels.*

EXCITING INSPIRATIONAL KITCHENS

The most exciting kitchens are a dynamic blend of *classic style* and *personal style.* So go ahead and mix, whether your taste is traditional, country or contemporary. Find inspiration at home in a treasured antique, a bright poster, travel souvenirs or grandmother's floral china. Here are a dozen stunning kitchens to get you started.

Photos pages 82 and 83 courtesy of Armstrong World Industries, Inc.

Regional style. *Southwestern galley kitchen tucked behind adobe fireplace mixes sleek European cabinets with rustic counters. Regional elements: rough ceiling beams, carved stool and plank shelving lined with copper cookware, baskets and earthy pottery.*

◀ ***Best of the Southwest.*** *Muted desert colors and Spanish-style whitewashed walls connect the living room and kitchen. Native Southwestern materials are abundant, such as leather chair, animal hide rug, handwoven blankets, steer horns and terra-cotta accessories.*

Borrow from the past

Capture an era with colors, patterns and furnishings from the past. For example, mimic a fifties kitchen, emphasizing chrome, metal cabinets and colors like aqua/black/white. Or, create a Victorian room with a palette of deep jewel tones and cabinets rich in decorative detail.

◀ ***Art Deco kitchen*** *has the bold outlines and streamlined look popular in the twenties and thirties. Deep green trims the pastel base cabinets and peach counters. Focal point: arched cabinets with graceful flowers.*

Photos pages 84 and 85 courtesy of WILSONART

Curved panel *joins sink cabinet and contemporary-style drawers. Art Deco designers experimented with new materials, like plastics. These high-gloss laminate cabinets and chrome-and-plastic drawer pulls are reminiscent of that tradition.*

Arched glass doors *extend above the cabinets to create a stunning look for this kitchen (far left). Dark cabinet interiors set off white tableware (above).*

Classic kitchens with updated styling

◀ ***New Orleans-style*** *great room is summertime cool in crisp white and sky blue. Garden greenery, lazy fans and louvered shutters define the romantic Southern look. The spice: triangular island that centralizes cooktop, sink, dishwasher and storage.*

Photos pages 86 and 87 courtesy of Armstrong World Industries, Inc.

Traditional redefined. *Light, natural finish and European overlay doors update the traditional raised-panel cabinets. More contemporary touches: white and tan tile, whitewashed range hood, pearly solid-surface counters, soaring cathedral ceiling.*

Strong colors, bold shapes

Silver stripes *shine against inky black. The steely bands flow across the room, changing from broad to narrow. Custom cabinet doors and appliance fronts are necessary to achieve the unbroken lines. The high-contrast materials and finishes create the dramatic look.* ▶

Square power. *The simple square is given the spotlight in this black and white kitchen. Squares appear in the checkerboard flooring, white ceiling and black ceramic wall tiles.*

White alcove *is set off by black ceramic tiles with red grout. The gentle arch of the alcove contrasts with the squares that dominate the kitchen's design.*

Photos pages 88 and 89 courtesy of WILSONART

Photo courtesy of Armstrong World Industries, Inc.

Dynamic colors unite three rooms *in this open-plan home. Kitchen colors are balanced; no single hue dominates. Black appliances contrast with white cabinets and bright yellow counters. Distinctive details: textured black walls, mini-tables, Oriental-style chairs, sliding doors.*

Simplicity in black

Photo courtesy of Tarkett Floors/WILSONART

Purely Oriental. *Traditional Japanese screens enclose an intimate dining area with mustard-colored walls. Lacquered dining table, red dishes and Oriental-style chairs enhance the Eastern theme. In the compact kitchen: black* shoji *screen, black cabinetry, black plate rack.*

American originals

▼ ***Spacious kitchen*** *blends turn-of-the-century charm with contemporary good looks. Old-fashioned details include painted cabinets, graceful hanging lamp, Palladian window and paneled ceiling. Brass range hood is set off by diamond-pattern ceramic wall tile.*

Photo courtesy of Crystal Cabinet Works, Inc.

Photo courtesy of WILSONART

Collector's kitchen *mixes 19th and 20th century design. Crisp white European cabinets are topped with a display of Americana. Antique pine refectory table complements the country hutch displaying heirloom china. The butcher-block island counter, pine cathedral ceiling and bleached flooring warm the white walls and cabinetry.*

Photo courtesy of WILSONART

Bare minimum: when less is more

Photos pages 94 and 95 courtesy of WILSONART

Neutrals *create a serene kitchen. Understated palette includes oyster island and cabinets, sandy ceramic tile, taupe refrigerator and gray walls. Glass block sparkles and walls turn silver under strategically placed recessed lights.*

◀ ***Essentials.*** *Ultrasleek kitchen bares its walls and virtually eliminates decoration. The result: contours of the distinctive island and overhead light panel have a big impact. Sink, cooktop, storage and serving bar are housed in the long, curved island. Unusual focal point: stairway silhouette.*